The Tao of Learning

Lao Tzu's Tao Te Ching Adapted
for a New Age

Pamela K. Metz

The Tao of Learning

Lao Tzu's Tao Te Ching Adapted for a New Age

Pamela K. Metz

Humanics New Age
Box 7400
Atlanta, GA 30309

Humanics New Age
Box 7400
Atlanta, GA 30309

PRINTED IN THE UNITED STATES OF AMERICA

Metz, Pamela
    The Tao of Learning/Pamela Metz.
        p.   cm.
ISBN 0-89334-222-X
1. Tao   2. Teaching   3. Lao-tzu. Tao te ching   I. Title
B127.T3M47 1993
371.1'02--dc20   93-1945
                                                       CIP

This book is dedicated to my teachers, students, friends, and family with appreciation and love.

Contents

Introduction 1

1   Meaning of *Tao* 3

2   Teaching Without Words 5

3   Not Doing 7

4   Foundations 9

5   Neutrality 11

6   Openness 13

7   Letting Go/Being Present 15

8   Authenticity/Flowing Like Water 17

9   Knowing When to Stop 19

10 No Expectations 21

11 Emptiness 23

12 Inner and Outer Vision 25

13 Success 27

14 Relaxing 29

15 The Teacher's Teachers 31

16 Sharing Power/Empowerment 33

17 Midwife Teacher 35

18 Order in Chaos 37

19 Being Centered 39

20 Teaching Wisdom 41
21 At One With the *Tao*...43
22 Paradox 45
23 Being Quiet 47
24 Trying Too Hard...49
25 Before the Beginning..51
26 Staying Grounded 53
27 Being Flexible...55
28 The Yin/Yang of Learning..57
29 A Time for All Things...59
30 Conflict in the Learning Environment.........................61
31 Discipline 63
32 Harmony..65
33 Know Thyself...67
34 Greatness...69
35 Simplicity 71
36 Strong and Weak..73
37 Doing Less 75
38 Exceptional Teaching..77
39 A Teacher's Power..79
40 Time Out..81
41 Good, Better, Best 83

42 Creating 85
43 Gentleness 87
44 Contentment 89
45 Being Foolish 91
46 Fear 93
47 Being in the Present 95
48 Non-interference 97
49 Trust 99
50 Beginnings and Endings 101
51 Connections 103
52 The Source 105
53 Possessions 107
54 Passing It On: Each One, Teach One 109
55 Like a Newborn Baby: Beginner's Mind 111
56 Integrity 113
57 Doing Less is Doing More 115
58 Unfolding: Being an Example 117
59 Moderation 119
60 Natural Process 121
61 Humility 123
62 Making Mistakes 125
63 Taking Risks 127

64 Life Cycles 129
65 Not Knowing: Theory and Practice 131
66 Teaching from the Back of the Classroom 133
67 Qualities for Learning: Simplicity, Patience, Compassion 135
68 Cooperation/Collaboration 137
69 Respect 139
70 Ordinary Wisdom 141
71 Not Pretending (Wounded Healer) 143
72 Inspiration 145
73 Courage to Decide 147
74 Grading (Natural Consequences) 149
75 Trust in the Learning Environment 151
76 Soft and Hard 153
77 Behind the Scenes 155
78 Being Gentle to Overcome 157
79 Failure As Opportunity 159
80 Freedom (Love) 161
81 Truthfulness (Natural Rewards) 163
Bibliography 164
Author's Note 165
Acknowledgements 165

x

Introduction

The Tao of Learning means how things happen in the learning process. Learning and teaching are about many things. Some of these "things" can be talked about, written about, observed, and evaluated. Other aspects of the learning and teaching processes are understood only through the direct experience of being in the roles of student and/or teacher. Through an adaptation of several English translations of Lao Tzu's *Tao Te Ching, The Tao of Learning* offers a nontraditional view of the many ways of learning and teaching. It is intended to inspire and nurture the reader. You can read this book from front to back as well as open it at random to receive guidance or to contemplate a problem or question.

1 Meaning of Tao

*T*ao means how things happen. The *Tao* of learning means how things happen in the learning process. The way of teaching that can be told is not the way that can be known.

What happens in the learning environment cannot be defined. What can be defined is not what happens in the learning environment.

Be aware of what is happening in the learning environment without trying. Be open to what is happening without judging. The *Tao* is how things happen.

2 Teaching Without Words

Everything in the world has its opposite. Each needs the other to exist: good and bad, full and empty, rich and poor, black and white.

Therefore, the wise teacher teaches without words and does without doing.

It is her environment, but she doesn't own it. When her work is finished, she moves on.

3 Not Doing

The wise teacher does not show off or give good grades for showing off. Competition and envy would grow.

The wise teacher teaches by not doing and by unlearning. She helps students let go of everything they thought they knew and asks questions of those who think that they know.

She practices not doing, so students will find their gifts.

4 Foundations

The *Tao* is not something you can touch. The *Tao* is like a foundation.

A foundation is used to support a structure but is not visible. *Tao* is the ground that supports the foundations of learning. *Tao* is the ground that supports the ground. Because of its depth and breadth, *Tao* makes learning and teaching infinitely possible and is never used up.

5 Neutrality

The *Tao* does not take sides; it knows both good and bad. The wise teacher does not take sides; she embraces all students in their goodness and badness.

The *Tao* is like the wind; it is empty, yet holds great power. The more you try to grasp it, the less you can hold.

When learning, stay close to your center.

6 Openness

The *Tao* of learning gives birth to 10,000 things; it is empty, yet full of life. The *Tao* is always present to be used however you like.

Only when you become closed to the infinite possibilities does the *Tao* become hidden.

7 Letting Go/Being Present

The teacher is present for her students, but she does not own them. They are not "her" students.

She serves them by letting go of herself. By letting go, she is present and fulfilled.

 15

8 ...Authenticity/Flowing Like Water

The student must be who he is. In the learning environment there can be no deception.

Obstacles provide a place of discovery – of energy, like water building up to flow around.

Let the natural flow of life be present in your learning; allow the unexpected and the unknown to appear without announcement. When this happens, the teacher and the taught can experience together that which is new to all of them.

9 Knowing When to Stop

Talk too much, and the students stop listening. Sit too long, and the students grow tired. Try too hard, and the way is lost.

Both the teacher and the students need to take time out from their learning and from each other. Distance provides perspective for returning to the work and to each other.

A wise teacher knows when to stop.

10 No Expectations

When you are teaching, can you remember why you began? Can you be flexible in the face of obstacles? Can you see clearly in your mind's eye even in the darkness of the unknown? Can you be gentle and guide others without directing them? Can you see the path, yet wait for others to discover theirs?

Learn to teach in a nurturing way. Learn to teach without possessing. Learn to help with no expectations.

Teaching without trying to control – this is a great challenge.

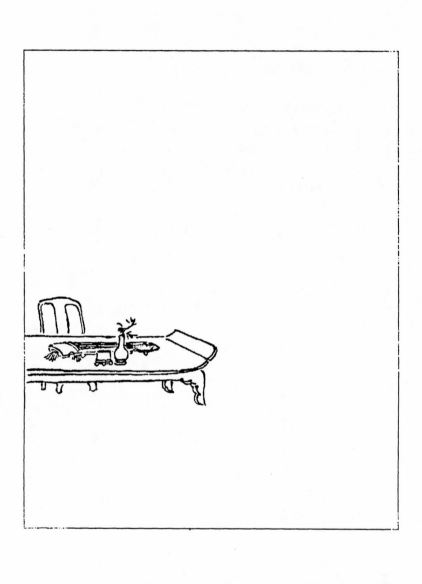

11 Emptiness

Spokes are joined together to make a wheel, but it is the hole in the middle that makes the wagon move.

Clay is shaped into a pot, but it is the emptiness inside that makes the pot useful.

Materials are assembled to make a school building, but it is the inner space of the classrooms that makes it possible for us to learn together.

Students work with forms and structures, but the emptiness and silence are also what we use for learning.

12 Inner and Outer Vision

To see what cannot be touched. To envision what is not yet realized. Lend a vision to students on their own paths to learning.

The wise teacher provides super-vision to point out some ways to possibility. The tension of inner learning and outer learning is essential for growth.

The teacher trusts her inner vision. She permits ideas to come and go. Her heart is as open as the sky.

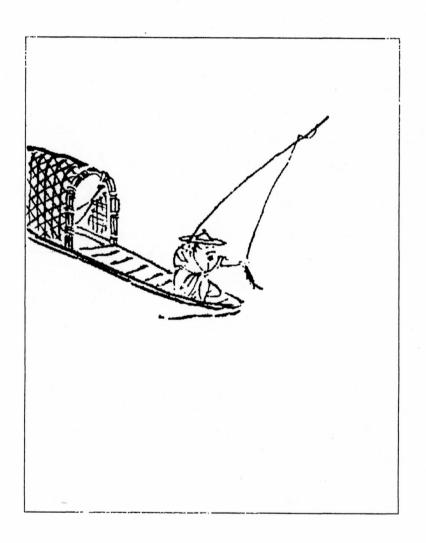

13 Success

In the learning environment the student must be careful of success. When others call your process a success, you may stop risking continued development.

It is important to remain detached from your good reputation. Hope and fear can keep your position off balance. Care for others as you care for yourself. Have faith in the process of growth. Then you can learn and still keep your balance.

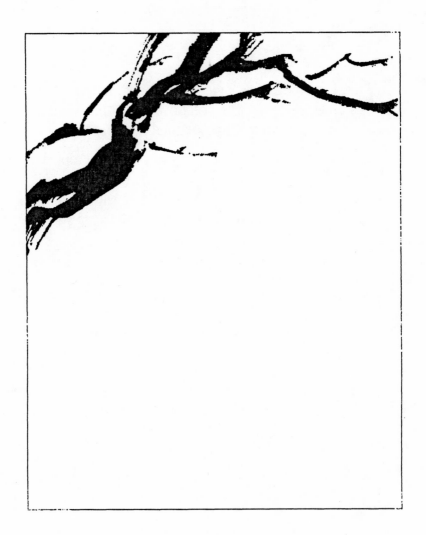

14 Relaxing

When you look, it can't be seen. When you listen, it can't be heard. When you reach for it, it can't be grasped. When what is happening in learning isn't clear, do not work too hard to figure things out.

Instead, relax and let your mind's eye see what is happening. Let your perceptions and intuition be your guides.

You can't know everything, but you can be open to the unknown and relaxed in the face of mystery.

When you are aware of the source of all things, you know the heart of wisdom.

15 The Teacher's Teachers

The teacher's teachers provided the models, but only the teacher can create her own path. The teacher waits to hear the students. She does not hurry them to her conclusions.

Fear should not dominate the learning environment. Learning in fear does not last. Children learn through play. Adults play to learn. Playfulness can be present even in serious learning.

16 Sharing Power/Empowerment

In learning, as in life, power must be shared. Learners and teacher together empower each other in the process of learning.

When students can work with partners, there is much to be gained. Each one then becomes a teacher and a learner, creating again the teacher and the taught.

When the teacher's work is complete, she is ready to stop.

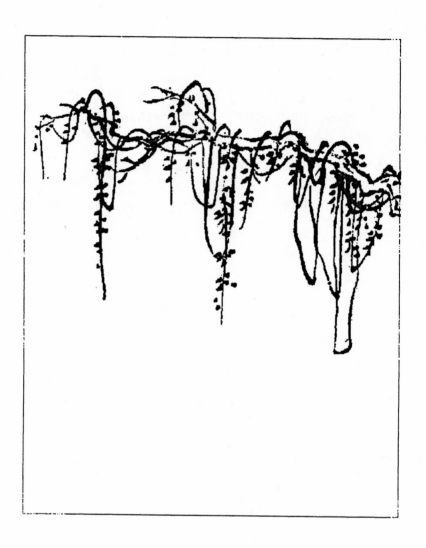

17 Midwife Teacher

When the wise teacher teaches, the students are hardly aware that she exists. Next best is a teacher who is loved. Next, one who is feared. The worst is a teacher who is hated.

If the teacher doesn't trust the students, they will not trust her. The teacher who assists at the birth of learning helps the students to discover for themselves what they knew all along.

When her work is finished, the students say, "Amazing! We did it ourselves!"

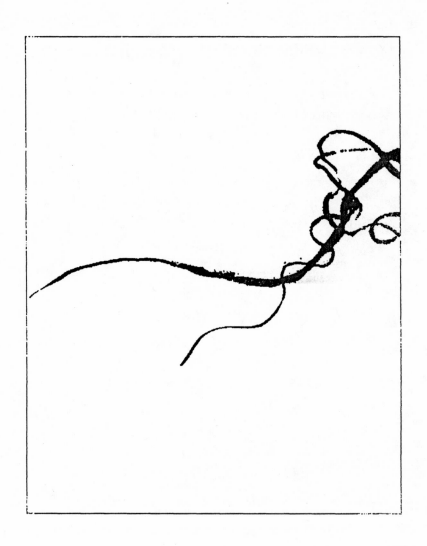

18 Order in Chaos

When the *Tao* of learning is forgotten, obedience and submission emerge.

When the students' intelligence diminishes, cleverness and deception increase. When there is no peace in the learning environment, pandering to the teacher develops.

When the learning environment is in chaos, the beginnings of order appear.

19 Being Centered

Eliminate superiority and arrogance, and the students will be happy. Throw away judgment and rules, and the students will do the right thing. Throw away busywork and grades, and there will not be any cheating.

If this is not enough, stay at the center of your environment and let the learning take its course.

20 Teaching Wisdom

Teaching takes the ordinary, the common, and in the translation creates something extraordinary. Only after the translation can the student understand how extra-ordinary teaching is.

Every day the teacher repeats those actions that lead to understanding. Chop wood, carry water every day. The teacher demonstrates simple tasks, which lead to simple truths.

Without routine, there is no learning. Without surprise, there is no wisdom.

21 At One With the Tao

That which gives you happiness is also the source of your sadness. Allow yourself to be free to experience the *Tao* of learning.

A teacher cannot go with her students; she can only point out the ways. After the departure, the students may return with news of their journeys.

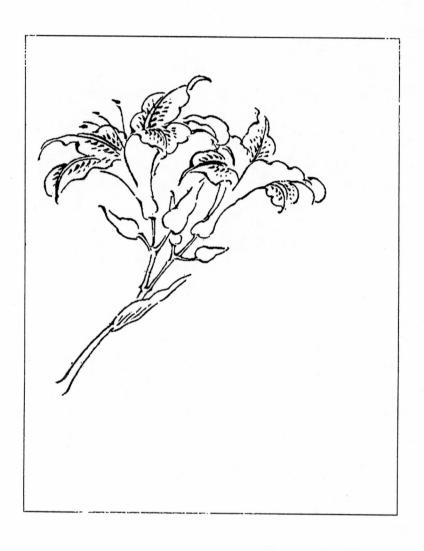

22 Paradox

The teacher's role is not the role of the students. The tension between the teacher and her students creates the yin and yang of learning.

If a teacher desires to be whole, she must become the parts. If she wishes to be straight, she must allow herself to be crooked. If she wishes to be full, she must allow herself to be empty. If she wishes to be reborn, she must allow herself to die. If she wants to receive, she must give everything up. The wise teacher, through the *Tao* of learning, becomes a model for her students.

Because she does not show off, students can enjoy her example. Because she has nothing to prove, students can trust her messages. Because she is without pretense, students recognize themselves in her. Because all things are possible, she is successful in her teaching.

When the early teachers said, "If you want to be given everything, give everything up," they were speaking truthfully.

When a teacher is with the *Tao*, she can truly be herself.

23 Being Quiet

Say what you have to say, and then be quiet. Be like the natural world: when it is blowing, it is the wind; when it is raining, it is only the rain; after the clouds move on, the sun shines through.

If you are open to the *Tao* of learning, you are in harmony and balance; you can embrace it totally. If you are open to reflection, you are clear and reflective; you can see completely. If you are open to loss and grief, you are at one with loss and grief; you can be accepting of the changes.

Be quiet and open to the *Tao* of learning. Trust your natural processes, and the puzzle will be complete.

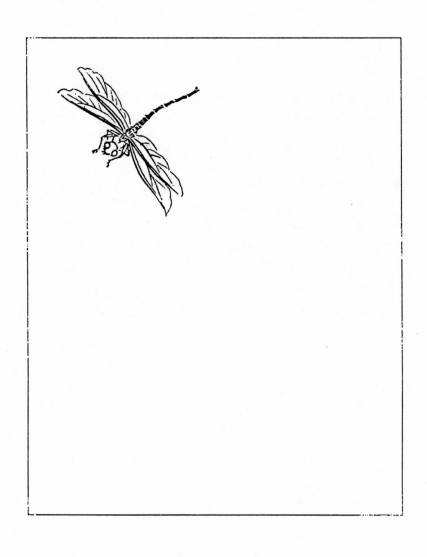

24 Trying Too Hard

If you stand on tiptoe, you will be off balance. If you go too fast, you won't go far. If you try to show off, you dim your own spotlight.

The student who defines himself doesn't really know who he is. The teacher who has power over others can't empower herself. The teacher who can't let go will create nothing that lives on.

If you want to know the *Tao* of learning, just do your job, and then let go.

25 Before the Beginning

Those who learn with us are part of the whole. Those who have learned before the beginning are also part. Those who learn after us complete the circle.

Only individual classes have beginnings and endings. True learning and teaching came before the beginning and will continue after the end.

26 Staying Grounded

The teacher who knows her roots can work with diffi-cult students without losing her balance.

Staying grounded means the teacher can travel all day without leaving the learning environment. In spite of the temptations, she stays calm in the face of conflict.

Why should the teacher be drawn into this argument or that? If she lets herself blow with the wind, she loses touch with her roots. If she becomes unstable, she loses touch with who she is.

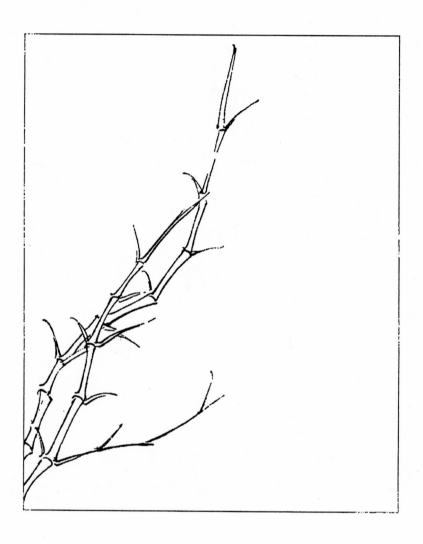

27 Being Flexible

A good teacher makes flexible lesson plans and is not solely intent on covering the material. A good teacher follows her intuition and lets it lead her through the lesson. A good teacher stays free of preconceptions and keeps her mind open to what is happening. The exceptional teacher is one who is accessible to all students and does not reject anyone. She is prepared to use emerging situations and is not wasteful. This is called being flexible.

Isn't a good student a bad student's teacher? Isn't a bad student a good teacher's challenge?

If this does not make sense, you will lose the way, no matter how many degrees you have.

This is the great mystery.

28 The Yin/Yang of Learning

Be aware of the male. Still, keep to the female; hold the world in your arms. If you embrace the world, you will be with the *Tao*, and you will be like an innocent child.

Be aware of the light. Still, keep to the dark; be a model for learning. If you are a model in the learning environment, you will embody the *Tao*, and you will know great freedom.

Be aware of the personal. Still, keep to the impersonal; accept all where they are. If you are accepting, you will embody the *Tao*, and you will return to your original self.

The learning environment is created from emptiness, like sculpture from a block of wood. The wise student is aware of the sculpture. Still, he values the block of wood. In this way, he can use all things.

29 A Time for All Things

Do you want to save the world? I don't think you can. The world is sacred. It cannot be saved. If you tinker with it, you'll ruin it. If you treat it like a thing, you'll lose it.

There is a time for getting ahead and a time for being behind; a time for moving, a time for rest; a time for being energetic, a time for being weary; a time for being careful, a time for throwing caution to the wind.

The wise student sees things in their natural state without trying to control them. He lets them go their own way while staying at the center of the circle.

30 Conflict in the Learning Environment

Whoever follows the *Tao* of learning doesn't try to force issues or defeat students by punishment. For every action there is reaction. Punishment, even when well-meaning, rebounds upon oneself.

The wise teacher does her work and then stops. She understands that much of the world is out of her control, and that trying to control everything goes against the *Tao* of learning.

Because she believes in her work, she does not try to convince others. Because she is content with herself, she does not seek others' approval. Because she accepts herself, others also accept her.

31 Discipline

Punishment is a tool of discipline; wise teachers avoid it. Punishment is a tool of fear; wise teachers use it sparingly and, if necessary, with great restraint.

Peace is of high value. If the peace has been broken, how can the teacher be content?

Her students are not enemies but human beings like herself. The teacher doesn't wish them harm, nor does she enjoy punishing them. How could she enjoy their failures and be pleased with their loss of control?

The wise teacher creates a learning environment with great compassion, a place where self-discipline is the goal.

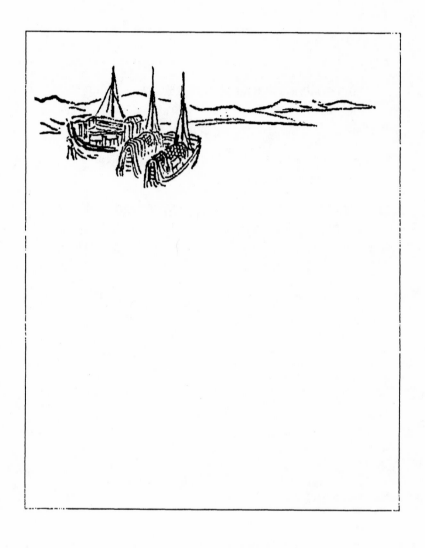

32 Harmony

The *Tao* of learning cannot be seen. Smaller than an atom, it contains innumerable worlds. If powerful teachers could be centered in the *Tao*, classrooms would be in harmony. Schools would be centered, people would be at peace, and rules would be followed.

When you use books and tests, know that they are temporary. When you have institutions, know when their functions should end. When you know when to stop, you can avoid danger.

Everything begins and ends in the *Tao*, just as streams and rivers flow into the sea.

33 Know Thyself

If you know others, you are intelligent; if you know yourself, you are wise. Having power with others is strength; having power over yourself is wisdom.

If you know how much is enough, you are truly wealthy. If you stay centered and embrace life and death with your whole being, you will live forever.

34 Greatness

The *Tao* of learning is everywhere. In the learning environment, all things come from it, yet it does not create those things. It is dedicated to its work, yet it does not boast. It nurtures students, yet it doesn't hold on to them.

Since the *Tao* of learning is a part of everything, it can be humble. Since everything merges into it and it endures all things, it could be considered great.

It isn't aware of this; therefore, it is truly great.

35 Simplicity

The student who is centered in the *Tao* of learning can go where he desires, without difficulty. He sees the big picture even when there is chaos, because he has a peaceful heart.

Songs and smells of good food make people stop and enjoy.

Words that describe the *Tao* of learning are plain and simple. When you look for the *Tao*, you cannot see it. When you listen for the *Tao*, you cannot hear it. When you use the *Tao* in the learning process, you cannot use it up.

36 Strong and Weak

When you want to decrease something, first allow it to grow. When you want to eliminate something, first allow it to flourish. When you want to possess something, first allow it to be given away. This is known as the awareness of the way things are.

The weak overcomes the strong. The slow overtakes the fast.

Let your learning remain a mystery. Let the results speak for themselves.

37 Doing Less

The *Tao* does nothing, yet through it all things are done. If exceptional teachers could center themselves in the *Tao*, their environments would be transformed by themselves in natural patterns.

Students would be content with the simplicity of their day-to-day lives, in harmony and free from desires. When there is no desire, the learning environment is peaceful.

38 Exceptional Teaching

The exceptional teacher doesn't try to be powerful; therefore, she is truly powerful. The ordinary teacher keeps reaching for power, and she never has enough.

The wise teacher does nothing, yet she leaves nothing undone. The ordinary teacher is always busy, yet much remains to be done. The kind teacher does something, yet something remains undone. The just teacher does something and leaves many things to be done. The moral teacher does something, and when students do not respond, she uses force.

When the *Tao* is lost, there is kindness. When kindness is lost, there is virtue. When virtue is lost, there is routine. Routine is a useless part of trust; routine can be the beginning of disorder.

Therefore, the extraordinary teacher is concerned with the whole and not a facade, with the fruit and not the blossom. She lives in the real world and lets go of illusions.

39 A Teacher's Power

When a teacher is in harmony with the *Tao*, the learning environment is clear and spacious, and the students are grounded and receptive. They all grow together and are pleased with their progress. They perform well and renew themselves.

When a teacher interferes with the *Tao*, the learning environment becomes crowded and the students become hostile; the balance is broken and possibilities are lost.

The wise teacher views all parts with compassion and hope, because she understands the whole. She consistently practices humility. She does not sparkle like a diamond but lets herself become as smooth and solid as a stone.

40 Time Out

Returning to one's center is the *Tao* of learning.
Taking time out is the *Tao* of learning.

All things come from existence. Existence comes from non-existence.

In the learning process, remember to take time out, to return to your center, and you will return to the *Tao* of learning.

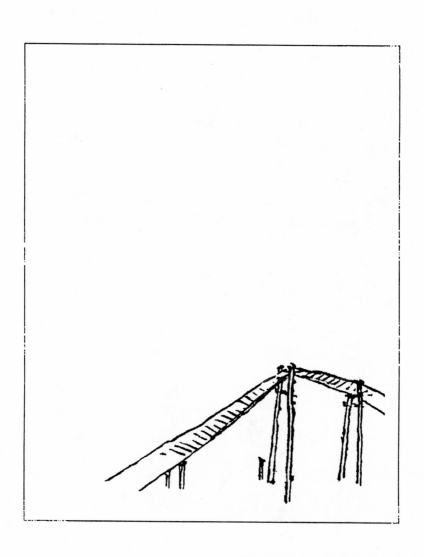

41 Good, Better, Best

When a wise teacher hears of the *Tao*, she quickly begins to embody it. When a good teachers hears of the *Tao*, she only half believes it. When a foolish teacher hears of the *Tao*, she ridicules it. If she didn't laugh at it, it wouldn't be the *Tao* of learning.

The story is told: the way to the light seems dark; the way ahead seems to fall behind; the short path seems long; strength seems weak; equality seems unfair; true dedication seems doubtful; true vision seems clouded; the best work seems inadequate; the greatest love seems uncaring; the greatest wisdom seems foolish.

The *Tao* of learning cannot be found, yet it nurtures and completes all things.

42 Creating

The *Tao* of learning gives life to One. One creates Two. Two gives birth to Three. Three creates everything.

Everything has creative possibilities. When polarities combine, there is harmony.

Ordinary students dislike solitude. The wise student makes good use of it, embracing his aloneness, being aware of his place in the universe.

43 Gentleness

The gentlest things in the learning environment overcome the hardest things in that environment.

That which has no substance can enter where there is no space. This shows the value of not acting.

Learning without words, doing without actions – this is the *Tao* of learning.

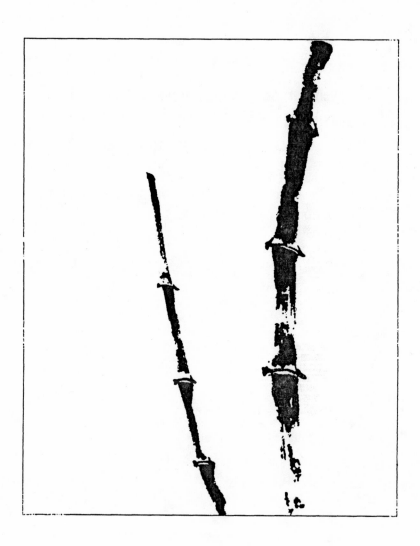

44 Contentment

Reputation or inner peace: which is more important?
Wealth or contentment: which is more valuable?
Winning or losing: which is more damaging?

If a student depends on others for contentment, he will
never be content. If his happiness depends on money,
he will never be happy with himself.

Be content with your world; celebrate the way things are.
When you understand that nothing is lacking, you can own
the whole world.

45 Being Foolish

True learning can be imperfect, yet it is perfectly itself. True completeness seems empty, yet it is fully finished.

The true path of life may be crooked. True wisdom seems foolish. True art seems artless.

The wise teacher permits things to unfold. She nurtures things as they happen. She steps aside and allows the *Tao* to speak for itself.

46 Fear

When the learning environment is in harmony with the *Tao*, the students excel. When the learning environment is not in harmony with the *Tao*, students are unproductive and fight with one another.

Fear is a great illusion. It causes the teacher and the students to defend themselves, creating winners and losers. If a teacher can dispel fear, the learning environment will be a safe place for everyone.

47 Being in the Present

Without opening the classroom door, the teacher can open hearts to the world. Without opening the windows, the students can experience the spirit of the *Tao*. The more you study, the less you understand.

The exceptional teacher becomes present without leaving, sees the light without looking, accomplishes without doing a thing.

48 Non-interference

When pursuing education, something is added every day. In the *Tao* of learning, something is unlearned every day.

The teacher needs to force learning less and less every day until finally she arrives at non-interference. When nothing is done, nothing is left undone. True learning can only be known by letting go or unlearning. It cannot be gained by interfering.

49 Trust

The exceptional teacher does not impose her will upon others. She works with the minds of her students. She is good to students who are good. She is also good to students who are not good. This is authentic goodness.

She trusts students who are trustworthy. She also trusts students who are not trustworthy. This is authentic trust.

The exceptional teacher's style is like the open sky. Students don't understand her. They respect her and remain open. She trusts students as if they were part of herself.

50 Beginnings and Endings

The wise student gives himself fully to the challenges of the learning process. He knows that everything ends and there will be nothing to hold on to: no deceptions in the mind, no reluctance in the body. He does not plan his actions; they come from the center of his existence. He holds nothing back from his learning; therefore, he is ready for anything, as a person is ready to rest after a full day of work.

51 Connections

*E*very student is an expression of the *Tao*. The *Tao* comes into being, unaware, complete, free, takes on physical properties and lets the life force complete it. That is why everyone can be in harmony with the *Tao*.

The *Tao* is the source of all things, nurturing them, caring for them, protecting them, and taking them back to itself.

The *Tao* of learning creates without owning, acts without expectations, guides without directing. That is why the *Tao* is the way of connecting with learning.

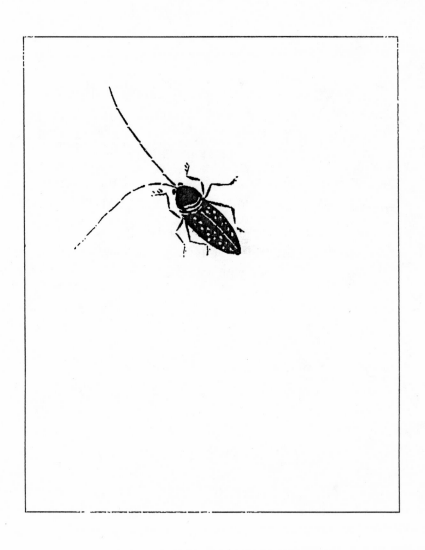

52 The Source

In the beginning was the source. Everything comes from it; everything returns to it.

To find the *Tao*, follow the path. When you identify the patterns and find your roots, you will understand.

If you close your mind and constantly judge your teachers, your heart will be heavy. If you keep your mind from judging and aren't deceived by appearances, you may find peace.

Being able to see when it is dark is perceptive. Being able to yield is strength. Be aware of your own light and return to its source. This is returning home.

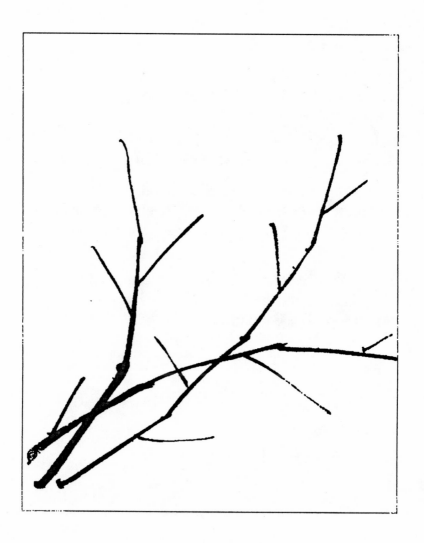

53 Possessions

The way of goodness is easy, but some students take the side paths. Be careful when things are out of balance. Stay centered within the *Tao*.

When wealthy bankers prosper while farmers lose their land, when government spends money on weapons instead of books, when the wealthy are extravagant and insensitive while the poor are without resources, it is criminal and disorganized. This is not in keeping with the *Tao*.

54 Passing It On:
Each One, Teach One

The teacher who is one with the *Tao* will not be displaced. The teacher who embraces the *Tao* of learning will not leave without saying good-bye. Her name will be respected from year to year.

Let the *Tao* be present in your learning, and you will become real. Let it be present in the classroom, and students will flourish. Let it be present in your school, and your school will be an example for other schools. Let it be present in your country, and there will be harmony.

How can this be true? Look inside yourself. Each one, teach one and then pass it on.

55 Like a Newborn Baby: Beginner's Mind

The student who is in harmony with the *Tao* is like a newborn baby whose bones are supple, whose muscles are soft, but who has a strong grip. It doesn't know how babies are made, yet its existence is evidence of the process. It can cry through the night without losing its voice.

The student's strength is like that of a newborn. He lets everything come and go without effort, without desire. He does not have expectations; therefore, he is not disappointed. Because he is never disappointed, his spirit stays young and hopeful.

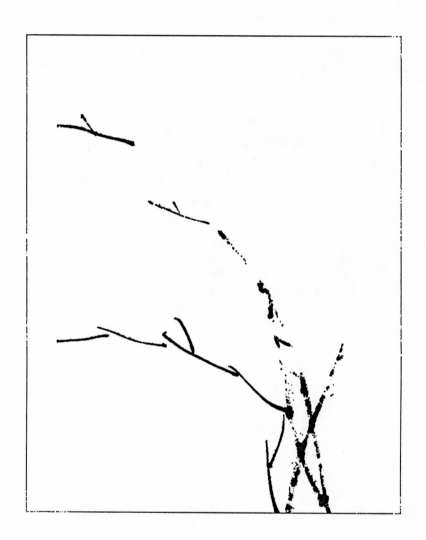

56 Integrity

Those who know don't talk. Those who talk don't know. Shut your mouth, muffle your senses, dull your sharpness, untie your knots, blur your sight, settle your accounts. This is the fundamental integrity.

Be like the *Tao*. It cannot be taken or given, promoted or defiled, honored or disgraced. It gives itself up again and again. That is why it survives.

57 Doing Less is Doing More

If you want to be an exceptional teacher, learn to follow the *Tao*. Stop trying to control; let go of predetermined plans and ideas. The learning environment will manage itself.

The more restrictions you give, the less compliant students will be. The more punishments you give, the less secure students will be. The more assistance you give, the less self-reliant students will be.

Thus, the wise teacher says: "I let go of the rules, and the students become honest; I let go of restrictions, and the students surpass my standards; I let go of reminding, and the students accomplish their tasks; I let go of desire for the common good, and the good becomes as common as stones."

58 Unfolding: Being an Example

If the learning environment is managed with acceptance, the students are relaxed and honest. If that environment is managed with repression, the students are difficult and mischievous.

If a teacher seeks power, the more the power, the more resistant the students. Try to make students happy, and you lay the foundation for discontent. Try to make students honest, and you lay the foundation for deception.

Therefore, the wise teacher is content to be an example and does not impose her power. She makes her point but doesn't push. She is direct but flexible. She is bright but easy on the eyes.

59 Moderation

For learning well, there is nothing better than moderation. The moderate student is free from his own
ideas.

He is as accepting as the sky, as consistent as the sunrise,
as solid as a mountain, as flexible as bamboo in a breeze.
He has no expectations in sight and uses whatever life
brings to his path.

Nothing is impossible for the moderate student, because
he has let go. He can care for his own well-being as loving
parents care for their children.

60 Natural Process

L earning is like frying a small fish. You can spoil it by doing too much poking.

Center your learning in the *Tao*, and difficulties will have no power. Not that there won't be difficulties, but you'll be able to step out of their way. Give difficulties nothing to confront, and they will disappear by themselves.

61 Humility

When a teacher develops great power, it becomes like the ocean: streams and rivers flow down to it.

The more powerful the teacher, the greater the need for humility. Having humility means trusting the *Tao* and not needing to be defensive.

A great school is like a great person: when it makes a mistake, it becomes aware of it; when it becomes aware of it, it corrects it; it considers those who give it feedback as its most important teachers. It thinks of its shadow as its own enemy.

If a classroom is immersed in the *Tao*, if it nurtures its students and doesn't concern itself with the affairs of other classrooms, it can be a model for the rest of the school.

62 Making Mistakes

The *Tao* is at the heart of learning. It is the good student's wealth, the bad student's safe harbor.

Awards can be won with words of praise. Respect can be had from outstanding work. But the *Tao* is beyond wealth, praise, or work, and no one can acquire it.

So, when a new student arrives, don't offer to help him with your wealth or your skills. Instead, offer to teach him about the *Tao* of learning.

Why did the first teachers value the *Tao*? When a teacher is one with the *Tao*, when she seeks, she finds; when she makes a mistake, she learns and is forgiven. That is why the *Tao* of learning is valued.

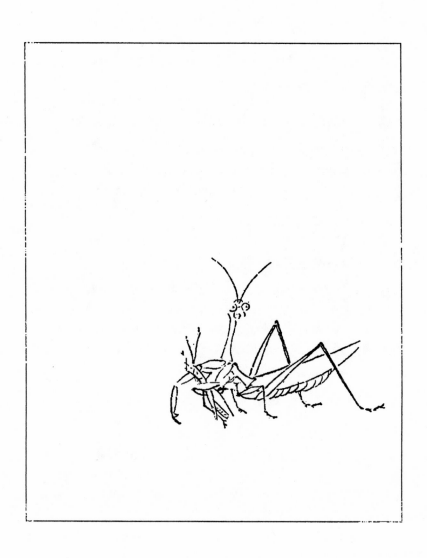

63 Taking Risks

Learn by being; work without strain. Consider the little to be big and the few to be many. Confront the challenges while they are manageable. Complete the whole by a number of small acts.

The accomplished student does not strive for perfection; therefore, he achieves perfection. When he runs into an obstacle, he stops and embraces it. He is not afraid of taking risks; therefore, there is nothing to fear.

64 Life Cycles

What has roots is easy to nurture. What is new is easy to change. What is rigid is easy to break. What is small is easy to scatter. Prevent difficulties before they happen. Put things in order before they are created.

The giant redwood grew from a small sprout; the journey of 10,000 miles begins by taking one step. Hurrying to action, you may fail. Holding on to things causes you to lose them. Rushing projects to completion, you destroy what is possible.

The wise teacher teaches by letting things take their course. She is as calm at the end as at the beginning. She has nothing; therefore, she has nothing to lose. What she wants is to want nothing. What she learns is to unlearn. She seeks to teach students about the gift of their humanity. She cares about the *Tao* of learning; therefore, she can care for all things.

65 Not Knowing: Theory and Practice

The ancient teachers didn't try to educate their students but gently taught them not to know.

When students think they know the answers, they are difficult to teach. When they know that they don't know, students can find their own way.

If you want to learn how to learn, avoid being arrogant or superior. The simplest way is the clearest. If you are content with an ordinary life, you can teach yourself the way to your own true nature.

66 Teaching from the Back of the Classroom

All water flows into the ocean, because it is lower than streams and lakes. Humility gives the ocean its power.

If you want to teach others, you must place yourself below them. If you want to lead, you must learn how to follow.

The wise teacher is above the students, and they do not feel oppressed. She leads the students, and they do not feel manipulated. They appreciate her. Because she does not compete with their performance in the learning environment, the students do not compete with her. She can teach from the back of the classroom.

67 Qualities for Learning: Simplicity, Patience, Compassion

There are those who say that the *Tao* of learning is nonsensical. Others label it idealistic and impractical. Those who seek to know themselves say that this nonsense makes sense. Those who can practice the *Tao* of learning are grounded in high ideals.

There are just three qualities for learning: simplicity, patience, compassion. These three qualities are the greatest gifts.

Simple in your process of learning and thinking, you return to the source of existence. Patient with enemies and friends, you acknowledge how things are. Compassionate with yourself, you make peace with the world.

68 Cooperation/Collaboration

The best teacher wants all teachers to teach well. The best leader can join with his followers. The best guide serves the people who are on the journey. The best student works with others in his learning environment.

All of them embrace the value of cooperation and collaboration. Not that they don't enjoy competition, but they work in the spirit of play. In this way they are like children and are in harmony with the *Tao*.

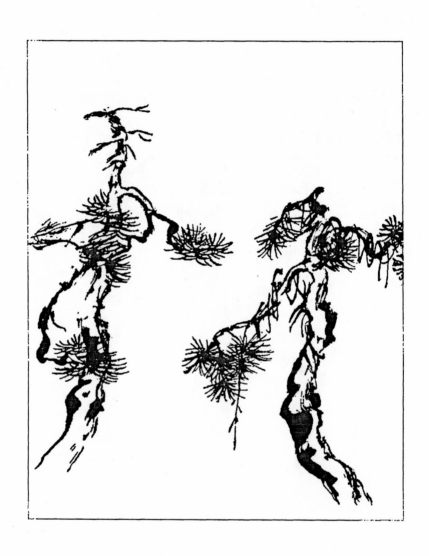

69 Respect

Experienced teachers say: "Instead of making the wrong move in the beginning, it is better to wait and see. Rather than pushing for a small gain, it is better to retreat a yard."

This is called moving ahead without advancing, gaining control without using threats.

There is no greater mistake than not respecting your students. Not respecting your students means thinking that they cannot learn; therefore, you destroy great potential and are not respected yourself. When students and teachers do not respect each other, success will come to the one who can give respect.

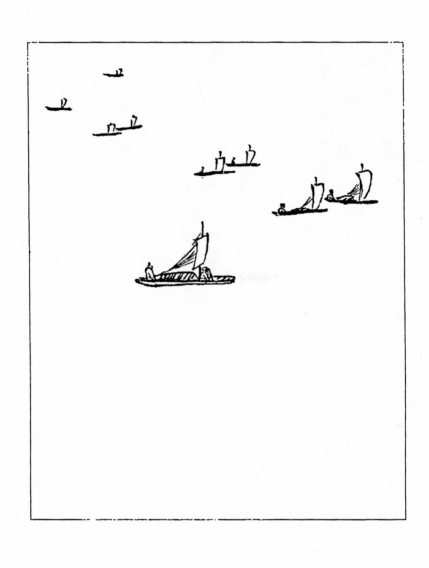

70 Ordinary Wisdom

The *Tao* of learning is easy to understand and easy to put into practice. Yet, your mind cannot grasp it and, if you try to imitate it, you will not succeed.

The *Tao* of learning is older than time. How can you find its meaning? If you want to know the *Tao* of learning, look inside your heart.

71 Not Pretending
(Wounded Healer)

Not to know is the beginning of truth. Pretending to know can be an obstacle.

First, realize that you are ignorant; then, you can begin to know.

The student is his own healer. When he knows that he does not know, then he is able to learn.

72 Inspiration

When students lose their sense of wonder, they begin to look for facts. When they cannot trust themselves, they begin to depend upon those in authority.

The wise teacher stays in the background so students will not be confused. She teaches without dogma, so that students will be inspired to keep their sense of wonder.

73 Courage to Decide

The *Tao* of learning is relaxed. It is courageous without competing, answers without speaking a word, arrives without being called, accomplishes without a plan.

Its scope is the whole world. And, although its view is wide, nothing goes unnoticed.

74 Grading (Natural Consequences)

If you are aware that all things change, there is nothing you will try to hold back. If you are not afraid of failing, there is nothing that you can't try.

Trying to control the students through grades is like trying to play a god. When you use someone else's tools, you may hurt yourself.

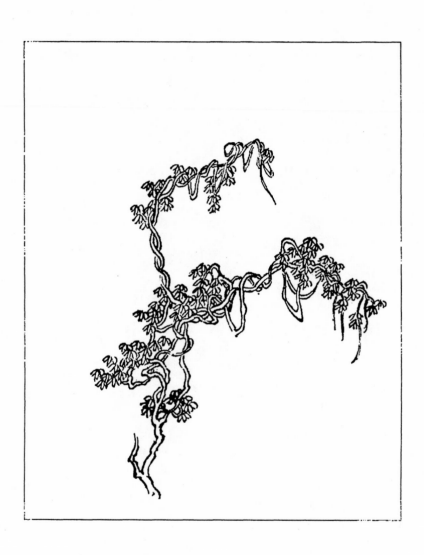

75 Trust in the Learning Environment

When rules are too harsh, the students rebel. When the environment is too controlling, the students lose their spirit.

Advocate for the students' benefit. Trust them; leave them alone.

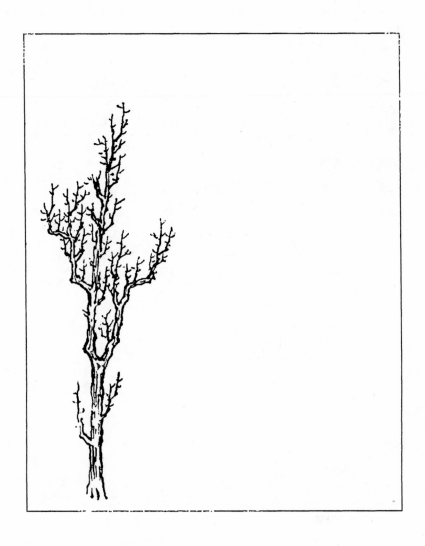

76 Soft and Hard

People are born soft and flexible; when they die, they become hard and brittle. Plants begin when they are tender and gentle; dead, they become dry and stiff.

Thus, when a teacher is hard and inflexible, she is a messenger of death. When she is soft and yielding, she is a harbinger of life. The hard and inflexible will break. The soft and yielding will persist.

77 Behind the Scenes

The teacher sets the stage for learning to happen. She does not try to control the students on their paths.

The teacher can continue to learn, because there is no end to the possibilities. She teaches without expectation, is successful without taking credit, and knows that she is no better than anyone else.

78 Being Gentle to Overcome

Water is soft and yielding, yet in its gentleness it overcomes the hard and unyielding.

The gentle teacher overcomes the hard students; the flexible teacher works with the rigid class. We know this to be true, but few can put this into practice.

The wise teacher remains calm even in the face of difficulties. Anger does not enter into her heart. Because she has given up helping, she is her students' greatest help.

Another paradox: gentle is strong.

79 Failure as Opportunity

Failing is an opportunity. If you blame another, there is endless blaming.

The wise teacher fulfills her role and models corrections of her own mistakes. She does what she needs to do and does not demand that others do this as well.

80 Freedom (Love)

In the love of learning and in the love of the learners, the *Tao* of learning is born. Freedom in learning and in teaching provides the possibilities.

If a classroom is managed wisely, the students will be content. They enjoy learning and don't waste time by acting up. Because they love their teacher, they are not interested in escaping. Because they love to learn, they find adventure and travel in the subject matter. Even though they may leave when the bell rings, they stay after class to continue their questioning. They are content to learn and so do not drop out of school.

81 Truthfulness (Natural Rewards)

The simple truth will suffice; fancy, complicated words are not necessary.

The wise teacher does not need to prove her points; those who need to prove their points are not wise. The wise teacher has no wealth. The more she helps students, the richer she is. The more she gives her knowledge to others, the greater is her reward.

The *Tao* of learning comes about by nourishing students in their natural pursuits. With learning not forced, the students learn.

Bibliography

Bolen, J.S. *The Tao of Psychology*. New York: Harper & Row Publishers, Inc., 1979.

Capra, F. *The Tao of Physics*. New York: Bantam Books, 1975.

Dreher, D. *The Tao of Peace*. New York: Donald I. Fine, Inc., 1990.

Feng, G.& J. English, trans. *Lao Tsu: Tao Te Ching*. New York: Alfred A. Knopf, Inc., 1972.

Fields, R. et al. *Chop Wood, Carry Water*. Los Angeles: Jeremy P. Tarcher, Inc., 1984.

Gibran, K. *The Prophet*. New York: Alfred A. Knopf, Inc., 1923.

Grigg, R. *The Tao of Being*. Atlanta, Georgia: Humanics New Age, 1989.

--------. *The Tao of Relationships*. Atlanta, Georgia: Humanics New Age, 1988.

--------. *The Tao of Sailing*. Atlanta, Georgia: Humanics Trade Paperbacks, 1990.

Heider, J. *The Tao of Leadership*. Atlanta, Georgia: Humanics New Age, 1986.

Hoff, B. *The Tao of Pooh*. New York: Penguin Books, 1982.

McGregor, J. *The Tao of Recovery*. New York: Bantam Books, 1992.

Mitchell, S. *Tao Te Ching*. New York: Harper & Row Publishers, Inc., 1988.

Suzuki, S. *Zen Mind, Beginner's Mind*. New York: Weatherhill, 1970.

Wing, R.L. *The Illustrated I Ching*. New York: Doubleday & Company, Inc., 1982.

--------. *The Tao of Power*. New York: Doubleday & Company, Inc., 1986.

Author's Note

The pronoun "she" is used throughout *The Tao of Learning* to refer to the teacher. The pronoun "he" is used to refer to the student. Both the masculine and the feminine voices are contained in each role, and the verses can be read with this in mind.

Acknowledgements

I am especially grateful to the following authors whose published works served as important sources for the development of this book: Stephen Mitchell (*Tao Te Ching*), R.L. Wing (*The Illustrated I Ching*), Jean Shinoda Bolen (*The Tao of Psychology*), Benjamin Hoff (*The Tao of Pooh*), Kahlil Gibran (*The Prophet*), Richard Fields et al. (*Chop Wood, Carry Water*), and Gia-Fu Feng and Jane English (*Lao Tzu: Tao Te Ching*).

My thanks also to Gary Wilson of Humanics Limited and to Carole Addlestone, who made a way for this book to take form.

Printed in the United States
2372